DON'T THROW ROCKS AT HIS WINDOW

DON'T THROW ROCKS AT HIS WINDOW

Real Advice to Mend a Broken Heart

JULIE C. DONALDSON

DESERET
BOOK

Salt Lake City, Utah

The true stories on pages 14, 19, 22, 28, 31, 40, 49, and 59 are used by permission.

Visit us at DeseretBook.com

Library of Congress Cataloging-in-Publication Data
Donaldson, Julie C.
  Don't throw rocks at his window : real advice to mend a broken heart / Julie C. Donaldson.
    p. cm.
    Summary: Using humor, common sense, and honest conversations, the author walks readers through the steps of not only surviving a broken heart, but also explains the process of learning to nurture strength in yourself and how to receive help from Heavenly Father.
    Includes bibliographical references.
  ISBN 978-1-60641-157-5 (paperbound)
  1. Separation (Psychology) 2. Forgiveness. I. Title.
HQ801.D693 2011
241'.6765—dc22   2010037580

Printed in the United States of America
R. R. Donelley, Crawfordsville, IN

10   9   8   7   6   5   4   3   2   1

To all the guys who broke my heart: I'm over you. Really.

And to Freddie, who captured it: Lucky us.

A BROKEN HEART AND A BAD CAR RIDE

I should have known something was wrong when Zack* offered to drive me home.

I lived across the street from him. Literally. Even though I throw like a girl, I could chuck a rock from my front porch and hit his bedroom window. (Not that I did that. Of course not.)

One day, after we'd been hanging out at his house, Zack said, "Hey, get in my car and I'll drive you home."

I laughed. What a kidder. It was just one of the things that I liked about him. We had gone on a few dates in the two months since he had moved onto my street, and we hung out at his house almost every weekend. The more time I spent with him, the more I liked him.

"No, really, get in," he insisted, and so I

1   *All names have been changed to protect the guilty.

got in his car and he drove across the street and stopped in front of my house.

I remember my mom and dad were out front working on the lawn.

A BROKEN HEART, NO MATTER HOW IT IS DELIVERED, HURTS.

Zack gripped the steering wheel and said, "I hope you're not letting me keep you from dating other people."

I stared at him, not understanding what was happening. Then I noticed the sinking feeling in my stomach and the heat spreading over my face and neck. My breakup sensor was beeping fast and loud. I couldn't believe it was happening like this. I looked out the window. He was breaking up with me in front of my house with my mom and dad standing ten feet away. This was awful.

"Can we talk somewhere else?" I asked.

Zack was nice enough to drive around the corner so he could finish breaking my heart without my parents looking on. Oh, he was very nice about it. He told me he thought that I liked him more than he liked me and that we should probably stop hanging out. He was so nice he even called me later to ask me if I had cried.

This was when I did not throw a rock at his window.

His being nice didn't lessen the pain of a broken heart, though. I still missed him. I still felt rejected. I still cried, even though I didn't want to. A broken heart, no matter how it is delivered, hurts.

Actually, the word "broken" doesn't do justice to how it really feels.

In a war movie, your heart would be the wounded soldier with his guts spilling out all over his hands.

On a cross-country car drive, your heart would be the roadkill.

In an art museum, your heart would be the Picasso painting that looks like a person was taken apart and then stuck back together with all the parts in the wrong places.

On a mission to Mars, your heart would be the astronaut who gets stranded outside of the space shuttle without a tether and goes floating off, silently screaming, to suffocate in cold, dark space.

Okay, enough with the painful analogies. Suffice it to say, a broken heart hurts. But it doesn't have to hurt forever. You can mend a broken heart. I no longer cry over Zack, or any of the other guys who broke my

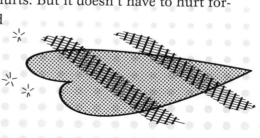

heart. I found healing, and even though it was a difficult road, I made it. And so can you.

So let's walk this mending road together, from despair to hope, from broken heart to mended heart, from an end to a new beginning.

COME ON, TRY IT! *(YOU'LL FEEL BETTER)*

WHAT DOES YOUR BROKEN HEART FEEL LIKE?

Make up your own analogy and draw a picture of it.

First Things First: Introductions

Since we are going to take this journey together, I believe introductions are in order. And, no, I don't mean I'll introduce myself to you. I want to introduce you to yourself.

If this were a book with a worldly perspective, I would tell you to go look at yourself in the mirror. But this is a book with a celestial perspective, and while "man looketh on the outward appearance," the "Lord looketh on the heart" (1 Samuel 16:7). I would have you see yourself the way the Lord sees you. If I could, I would take away all your earthly trappings, both good and bad. I would erase the natural man or woman, healthy or sick, strong or weak, handsome or homely. Then I would show you the radiant, glorious, magnificent spiritual being that you are.

Not were. Not will be. *Are.*

You don't remember this, but I have it on good authority that you once walked with God, the Creator of the universe, and He saw infinite potential within you. Among the billions of people who have lived on this earth, you are a member of the finest generation, held in reserve for these last days. Out of all of God's children, you are among His strongest, noblest, and most valiant.

> YOU ARE A RADIANT, GLORIOUS, MAGNIFICENT SPIRITUAL BEING. NOT WERE. NOT WILL BE. ARE.

In fact, you were probably among those who were mentioned by Abraham when he said, "Now the Lord had shown unto me, Abraham, the intelligences that were organized before the world was; and among all these there were many of the noble and great ones; and God saw these souls that they were good, and he stood in the midst of them, and he said: These I will make my rulers" (Abraham 3:22–23).

You might want to write that scripture on a piece of paper and tape it to your mirror, but even if you don't, I do hope you will write it in your heart. I want you to understand that you have the potential to one day be like God, with thrones, kingdoms, principalities, powers, dominions, and exaltations (see D&C 132:19). You will be more glorious than you can now fathom. That potential to be like God is within you right now, just like a tiny seed has within itself all of the potential to grow into a great tree, or a flower, or a squash plant. ← *The best kind of squash plant.*

So I want you to keep in mind your true identity as well as your eternal potential as we work together to mend your broken heart. When I tell you that some actions are beneath you, this is what I mean: that as one of the finest and most glorious of all of God's creations, you owe it to yourself and to Him to be the best version of yourself that you can be.

Doctor, Ain't There Somethin' I Can Take?

Have you ever had a scab that you picked at over and over again? What happens every time you pick it off before the wound is completely healed? You have to wait for a new scab to grow and for the wound underneath it to heal. You set back your healing time every time you do it.

A broken heart can feel as real as a physical wound. In fact, if you think of it as a wound and treat it as a wound, you will be on the right path for healing. Picking at the wound in your heart will only set back your healing time. It needs to be left alone, and it needs time to heal.

In Jane Austen's story *Emma*, Mr. Knightley and Emma are talking about Frank

Churchill's secret engagement to Jane Fairfax. Mr. Knightley is under the impression that Emma is in love with Frank. So he, in a very sympathetic, but unfortunately cheesy way, says, "Time will heal your wound."

But she's not! She's in love with you, Mr. Knightley! YOU!

That line always makes me laugh, but there is truth to it. Time *will* heal your wound. Time will bring with it a dulling of the ache and a lessening of the sting. The pain of loss and rejection will subside, little by little, if you do not interfere. Every day can bring you a little bit closer to having a mended heart.

> **THE PAIN OF LOSS AND REJECTION WILL SUBSIDE, LITTLE BY LITTLE, IF YOU DO NOT INTERFERE.**

But you have to leave it alone! No scab-picking allowed. And as you give your heart time to heal, there are some rules of recovery that will help you on your way.

RULE #1

DON'T BE PATHETIC

Don't be pathetic. If you have behaved pathetically in the past, don't worry—we'll keep that to ourselves. But today is the day to turn over a new leaf. Here are some of the most common pathetic behaviors that you must avoid from now until forever:

1. Wallowing in misery.

2. Singing along to breakup songs.

3. Going out in public wearing your dad's sweatpants and smelling like you haven't bathed in five days.

4. Begging him to take you back.

WALLOWING IS GOOD FOR BARNYARD ANIMALS, BUT NOT FOR PEOPLE

Feeling sad is a natural part of having a broken heart. It's easy to think that because you're sad now, he must have made you happy before. But *he* did not make you happy. You *decided* to be happy with him, and you can decide to be happy without him. You might always feel the pang of losing that relationship, but you do not have to bathe in misery like a pig wallowing in mud. You have control over how sad you feel, and for how long.

> YOU HAVE CONTROL OVER HOW SAD YOU FEEL, AND FOR HOW LONG.

Since this book is about healing a broken heart, I should, in good conscience, tell you not to wallow at all. But since you will probably disregard that advice anyway, I will give you permission to go ahead and wallow for one day. Just one!

If you've already had your day, you don't get another one now. If you've had more than one day . . . well, I'll let it slide, just this once. But if you just got your heart broken, you are allowed *one* day.

> **Q:** Why *do* pigs wallow in mud?
>
> **A:** To keep cool, because they don't sweat. You, on the other hand, do sweat. So no wallowing.

I'll cover my eyes now while you wallow. Just don't tell me about it. ↗ All done? Great. Nothing wastes time like wallowing.

Here's the thing: wallowing will not help you mend your broken heart. Wallowing is a self-indulgent pity party where nobody has any fun, especially not you. It will only increase your misery and the time it takes you to heal your broken heart. So leave the wallowing to the pigs, and decide today to be happy.

OINK.

13

TRUE STORY!

I had dated this guy and was feeling pretty good about where things were going when he called me one night and asked me to come over, where he promptly broke up with me.

Then he said, "Before you leave, can I have one last kiss to always remember you by?"

Disgusted, I said no and immediately left his house. Moments later he sent me a text that said, "I forgot to tell you while we were dating that I love you."

—J. B.

BREAKUP SONGS HAVE
TERRIBLE LYRICS

Please do not sing along to sappy love songs while crying your eyes out. First of all, crying for long periods of time will give you a headache. If this happens, it's because you have lost all of the water in your body through your tear ducts. You will need to stop crying and drink at least two full glasses of water, okay?

Second, listening to music that makes you cry is all part of wallowing, which, as we've already mentioned, doesn't help.

Finally, have you ever paid attention to the lyrics of breakup songs? How is the line "I can't breathe without you" supposed to help you mend your broken heart? It's not. It's self-indulgent pity-partying at its worst.

I love music, but music is

powerful. It can manipulate your emotions for good or for bad. A really gut-wrenching love song can make you feel more wretched than you already do on your own.

Besides that, chances are good that the people who live with you will hear you, and trust me, nobody with a whole heart actually likes to listen to sappy love songs accompanied by crying all day. And you need the people around you to have as much patience with you as possible because mending a broken heart can be a hard process.

> MUSIC IS POWERFUL. IT CAN MANIPULATE YOUR EMOTIONS FOR GOOD OR FOR BAD.

So if you need—really *need*—to listen to a gut-wrenching song, here is what you can do. Find a place where nobody else can see you—under a bed, in a closet, or behind the food storage. Go inside that little place with your headphones and let yourself feel the heartbreak of a really good love song. You can even let yourself cry a little. And then stop. Stopping is the important part here. A little self-indulgence can be cathartic. A lot of self-indulgence is wallowing, which is not allowed. So do it only a little.

The rule is that after you listen to one gut-wrenching song, you have to listen to an uplifting song. It can be a song that makes you want to dance or go for a run. It can be something religious that helps you feel the Spirit. But the important thing is to end your music session with a song that makes you feel good.

Then crawl out of your hiding place and face the world again with dry eyes. You can be happy without him. You really can. You can have a full, purposeful life without him. Just give yourself some time to heal and then watch your great life begin.

COME ON,
TRY IT!
(YOU'LL FEEL BETTER)

LIST FIVE SONGS THAT HELP YOU FEEL UPBEAT AND HAPPY:

_____

_____

_____

_____

_____

CHANGE THE WORDS TO YOUR FAVORITE SAD SONG TO CREATE AN "UN-BREAKUP" SONG:

(Example: "I can't live, if living is without ~~you~~ shoes.")

_____

_____

_____

_____

_____

_____

TRUE STORY!

We met in our college photography class, and after much flirting in the darkroom, he finally asked me out. We went out twice and had a great time. After the second date he gave me a burned CD of semi-romantic songs that we'd listened to together, and I figured he must really, really like me. Later, I learned that it was his way of telling me, "I had a great time, but I don't want to date you again."

—H. W.

THE DANGER OF LETTING YOURSELF GO

Please don't go out in public looking like you just rolled out of bed. You see, it's a small world, and you could run into anyone. You could run into your neighbor, who might have a nephew who's coming to visit for the summer and who might be the greatest thing to ever walk your street. He might be the one to make you wonder why you ever cared about what's-his-name in the first place. And you certainly do not want to look like leftover meatloaf the first time you meet him.

> **YOUR BODY AND MIND AND SPIRIT ARE INSEPARABLY CONNECTED, AND WHAT YOU DO TO ONE AFFECTS THE OTHER.**

What's even more likely is that you will see *him*. You might even see *him* with the new girl he's dating.

You know, the heartbreaker.

20

And she will be wearing makeup and her hair will be styled because she wants to impress him. Imagine if you were to go to the grocery store wearing your dad's sweatpants and you bumped into *him* and *her.* You would want to die from embarrassment. And, come on, nobody wants you to die from embarrassment.

But the importance of taking care of yourself actually goes deeper than avoiding potential embarrassment. Your body and mind and spirit are inseparably connected, and what you do to one affects the other. So when you take care of your body by exercising, eating well, and showering on a regular basis, your mind and spirit will also feel energetic, healthy, and clean.

The opposite is true, as well. If you spend your days eating cookies in a dark room while watching soap operas for hours, your mind and spirit will feel dark and junky. That will not help you feel better, and it will not help you progress on your road to a mended heart. So, get up early, exercise, shower, look your best, and greet the world with a smile. You will feel better when you do. I promise.

TRUE STORY!

After we had been dating for six months, he said he "liked" me a lot, but he wasn't sure he was ready for a "big commitment." He thought it would be best for both of us to "date around for a while."

I never heard another word from him again.

Five months later, I saw his wedding announcement in the newspaper.

—S. B.

NO SELF-RESPECTING GIRL BEGS TO BE TAKEN BACK

There will be no begging allowed. Do not talk to him while you're crying about how hurt you are. Do not ask him to give you another chance. Do not threaten to throw yourself off a cliff if he doesn't swear his undying love for you. These are all actions of a desperate person, and you are not desperate. So don't act desperate, and don't make him pity you. It won't change his mind or his heart, and in the end you will only feel embarrassed that you gave up your dignity.

I had a roommate in college who called her ex-boyfriend, crying and begging him to give her

> YOU DESERVE TO BE WITH SOMEONE WHO WANTS TO BE WITH YOU.

another chance. He came over, they talked, and she was suddenly smiling and happy and cooking dinner for him. He, on the other hand, looked like he wanted to run screaming from the room. The relationship lasted only one day, and then they were back to square one, with her crying and him running and screaming.

You deserve to be with someone who wants to be with you. And you will find someone who feels that way. In the meantime, keep your dignity and your self-respect.

Now, there are many other ways for a person to be pathetic. I won't list them all here. But before you do something in regard to your ex, ask yourself, "Is this pathetic? Will I feel worse about myself? Will others respect me less if I do this?" If the answer is yes, then don't do it.

RULE #2

Don't Be Creepy or Neurotic

This rule is very simple. Don't be creepy! Don't be neurotic! Here are a few particulars, since people who are prone to strange behavior often don't recognize that they are behaving in a creepy or neurotic way:

1. Do not stalk your ex.

2. Do not stalk your ex's relatives.

3. Do not damage something belonging to your ex (his car, his house, his kneecaps).

4. Do not behave like a fictional character.

STALKING IS FOR
PREDATORY ANIMALS

First of all, let's define stalking.

v. stalked, stalk·ing, stalks
1. To pursue by tracking stealthily.
2. To follow or observe (a person) persistently, especially out of obsession or derangement.

GGRRR...

Did you catch that? Obsessed and deranged people stalk other people. Are you supposed to be obsessed? Are you supposed to be deranged?

No! A thousand times, no!

Here's the thing: you have to plan on living the

rest of your life without him. Yes, some people break up and get back together, but it rarely ever lasts. It's better to move on after the first breakup, and stalking is the opposite of moving on.

> THE ACTIONS OF A DERANGED, OBSESSED PERSON ARE BENEATH YOU.

So, don't drive by his house to see if he's there or not, or who might be there with him. Do not shine your bright headlights on his front porch to catch him kissing his new girlfriend. It will not make you feel better, and it will not help you heal. These are the actions of a deranged, obsessed person, and they are beneath you.

And besides that, restraining orders can really be a pain.

I was in my last year of college and was dating someone seriously; we were even talking about getting married. After my last exam, I went to my girlfriend's apartment to celebrate. Her roommate—who didn't like me much anyway—answered the door and told me my girlfriend had gone home. It took me a moment to realize she meant *home*—as in three states away. A few months later, I received an apology letter.

—P. A.

RELATIVES WILL NOT HELP YOUR CAUSE

It doesn't matter if his mom loves you and named her parakeet after you. It doesn't matter if his grandmother pinched your cheek and declared your hips perfect for bearing his future children. It doesn't matter if his younger brother thinks you're cool because you kick the soccer ball around with him. None of that will make one bit of difference in that boy's heart, so leave the relatives out of it.

In some cases, talking to his relatives can actually make things worse. Remember Zack—the one who broke up with me in his car? I'm embarrassed to admit this, but I had talked to his mom about him the day before. I knew that she liked me, and I said something to her about

TWEET, TWEET!

how I liked Zack and I wished I knew if he liked me as much as I liked him. And why wasn't he asking me out on more dates?

So the next day, when Zack told me that he thought I liked him more than he liked me, I knew exactly who had given him that information. Instead of helping my cause, his mom had made it worse! I learned a valuable lesson that day, which I will pass on to you: if he doesn't want you on his own, there is no way anyone else will make him want you.

> **IF HE DOESN'T WANT YOU ON HIS OWN, THERE IS NO WAY ANYONE ELSE WILL MAKE HIM WANT YOU.**

And, honestly, you deserve to be loved by someone who just plain loves you for who you are, without interference or pressure or stalking or manipulation. Don't worry—there will be other boys, and other moms, and other parakeets.

TRUE STORY!

It was perfect! We had been dating for three-and-a-half months and even had our first kiss on New Year's Eve. Then, out of nowhere, he told me we should both start dating other people, and that while I was *probably* "the one," he needed more time before he could think about getting married. When I told him that I loved him, he told me that I "couldn't possibly know that for sure after only three-and-a-half months."

He married the next girl that he dated after me, proposing after they'd been together for only three-and-a-half months.

—A. R.

YOU BREAK IT, YOU BUY IT

Please do not cause damage to him or to his possessions. Don't egg his car or toilet paper his house. You might feel a teeny bit better while the egg is leaving your hand, and maybe even when you hear it go *splat*, but later you will recognize what a small, hateful act it was, and then *you* will feel small and hateful too.

My husband told me that he once had to turn down a girl who had asked him to a dance. He had gone to the previous dance with her, and his mom was concerned about them getting too serious too fast. Of course, the girl was disappointed. But the next day she sent him a bunch of suckers with a note attached that said, "Sucker! You thought I really wanted to go with you."

Oh, please do not ever do something like that. It's better to be secretly disappointed than to strike back at the person that you like (or liked) and try to make him feel bad about himself. It won't fool him, you know. But it will make him think less of you. And it's mean.

In a desire to strike back, you might also feel tempted to speak badly about him to your friends, his friends, or anyone who will listen. Not only will that not really make you feel better, it will actually harm you. It will make you feel small and petty. Plus, you will force your mutual friends to choose between the two of you—and they might not choose you.

> VENTING YOUR NEGATIVE FEELINGS WILL NOT RELEASE THE NEGATIVITY WITHIN YOU.

Contrary to popular opinion, venting your negative feelings will not release the negativity within you. No matter how often you vent about him, and no matter how many people agree with you about what a toad he is, you will still feel bad. All you will accomplish by talking badly about him is to pollute the air around you.

And consider this: if other guys hear you talking trash about your ex, do you think they'll want to ask you out? They will probably be afraid of what you'll say about *them* if they ever ask you out and it doesn't work out between you. Bottom line: there is no way talking badly about your ex will help you.

Sometimes stores display the sign "You break it, you

buy it." Well, you can't actually *buy* your ex's broken kneecaps, but the principle is the same. You will be stuck with the consequences of your actions, and nothing good can come from harming someone else.

If you really need to damage something, go ahead and rip out the blank page following this one and tear it to shreds. Or chew it up and spit it out. Or scribble on it. Or draw a picture of your heartbreaker looking like a terrorist, or a ballerina. Or a terrorist doing ballet. Do whatever you want to that page.

But no swearing. I didn't swear once in this book, so please don't ruin it for me.

YOU ARE NOT A FICTIONAL CHARACTER, SO DON'T BEHAVE LIKE ONE

The last of my warnings is this: do not behave like a fictional character. Fictional characters often do things that you should never do. A girl who is left by a vampire might go catatonic for a week and then sink into a soul-sucking depression and do nothing but stare out of a window for months, but you are not allowed to do that. You are not a fictional character.

And trust me, if you did behave like that, there would be no hot werewolf with killer abs waiting to fall madly in love with you. There wouldn't even be a dorky, kind of cute human boy hoping you'd notice him. There would only be a mental ward in a hospital, medicine, and thousands of dollars worth of therapy awaiting you.

Have you heard the expression "like attracts like"? It means that happy people attract other happy people. Angry people attract other angry people. Successful people attract other successful people. In this case, the rule of opposites attracting doesn't apply. Angry people do not attract happy people. Neurotic people do not attract normal people.

> HAPPY PEOPLE ATTRACT OTHER HAPPY PEOPLE.

So be sane. Be normal. It's a much better place to be than in a straightjacket.

COME ON, TRY IT! (YOU'LL FEEL BETTER)

WHAT QUALITIES ARE YOU LOOKING FOR IN A BOYFRIEND?

_____

_____

_____

_____

_____

WHAT QUALITIES DO YOU THINK YOUR IDEAL GUY WILL LOOK FOR IN A GIRLFRIEND?

_____

_____

_____

_____

_____

(Hint: They might be the same.)

TRUE STORY!

We had been dating for about six months. Before our date, I had been asked to swing by the bishop's office to chat about a new calling. While we were sitting there waiting, she started to give me the "It's not you, it's me" speech—she was dumping me!

When we left the bishop's office, the counselor asked me, with a meaningful glance at my girlfriend, if I might not be single for much longer. I assured him that I would be.

I still took her to the movies, though. Awkward!

—D. K.

BE BETTER THAN YOU'VE BEEN BEFORE

Now that we've covered the basic rules of what <u>not</u> to do, let's talk about some of the important things you <u>can</u> do to help mend your broken heart:

1. Avoid jealousy.

2. Be kind to yourself.

3. Draw closer to God.

4. Forgive the one who hurt you.

5. Apply the Atonement.

JEALOUSY: IT'S LIKE JUMPING INTO A VAT FILLED WITH FLESH-EATING BACTERIA

If the guy who broke your heart starts dating someone new, you will probably feel one of two things:

One—You can't believe he likes her! There is no way she's cuter than you!

She's a dog. She's worse than a dog. She's a dog with hoof-and-mouth disease.

Two—You can't believe he got such a beautiful girl to go out with him. It's like a kick in the teeth. It's like finding out that the only reason he broke up with you is because of your looks. It's so humiliating.

Please don't believe either of these things. Don't compare yourself to anyone else. That boy is not your judge and jury. He is one person looking for someone to love. You might not be right for him, but that doesn't mean that you are not right.

I once had a bad crush on a guy named Taylor. He

was a drummer—a really cute drummer—and we were in the same music class at college. I loved him from afar. After crushing on him for months, I did something courageous and asked him if he wanted help studying for the final. He didn't even know my name at the time, but he was struggling in the class, so he took me up on my offer.

> YOU MIGHT NOT BE RIGHT FOR HIM, BUT THAT DOESN'T MEAN THAT YOU ARE NOT RIGHT.

As I got to know him, I realized that he was even better than I had imagined him to be—so cute and funny and sweet. When we studied together I made him laugh. He drove me home for Christmas break (no small favor—four hours there and four hours back) just because I didn't have a ride. I was sure he liked me.

After I helped him pass the class, I asked him to go on a group outing to play in the snow, and he held my cold hands in his to warm them up. (He held my hands! He liked me!) I knew his class schedule and where he lived, and I started placing myself in strategic locations so he could run into me several times each day. It wasn't really stalking—I was just giving him lots of opportunities to see me and discover that I was the one for him. ⟵ Right?

I asked him out a couple more times, and he always

seemed to have a great time, but I gradually started to notice that he never asked me out. And then I noticed that he had another admirer. I knew who she was because she was also a music major. Her name was Desiree. And she played the harp. She had long blonde hair that tended to cascade around her shoulders. She looked like an angel.

I quickly grew to hate Desiree.

Whenever I saw her, I felt vastly inferior in the looks department. And sometimes when I was stalking—I mean *walking*—with Taylor, we would run into Desiree. She would call out to Taylor, and he would stop and talk to her. They would talk and talk, and I would start to feel really dumb just standing there, since she never acknowledged my presence. Eventually, I would realize that Taylor had forgotten I was there, and I would walk away.

Um, pathetic much? Yeah.

I grew desperate. I took him cookies, only to learn that Desiree had baked him cookies that day too. And then one night I called him to see what he was doing, and he told me he was going on a date with Desiree.

Did hers taste better than mine? Probably.

FLESH-EATING BACTERIA

There doesn't have to be a formal breakup for a heart to

be broken. Sometimes the worst heartache comes after learning that the person you like doesn't like you back. I liked Taylor so much, but I realized that he was never going to like me as much as I liked him. I was filled with jealousy and bitterness and anger. I felt like I was swimming in a vat filled with flesh-eating bacteria. It ate at me, day and night, and I could hardly think of anything else.

Can you actually fill a vat with flesh-eating bacteria? I'm no scientist, but I would guess probably not. Like all bacteria, it's microscopic. But you could fill the vat with some liquid, like, say, lemon juice, and then contaminate it with the flesh-eating bacteria, and then fall into it. That would definitely work.

One day Taylor was late getting to band. He passed me in the hall, shoved a dollar at me, and said, "Go get me a muffin from the vending machine."

I looked at that dollar and something changed inside of me. My anger toward Desiree switched to Taylor. I felt used, and I did not like it one bit.

Well, I got the muffin. It cost seventy-five cents. I carefully unwrapped the plastic wrap, shoved the spare quarter inside the muffin, and wrapped it back up, so that it looked perfectly normal. When I took it to Taylor in the band room, I delivered it with a stomp on his bare foot.

Later, he asked me what the stomp was for.

"For telling me to get you a muffin," I said.

"A muffin with a quarter in it!"

Hah! So he had found it! I hoped he had chipped a tooth on it.

Things went downhill from there, as you can probably guess. I had no hope of Taylor liking me because I had stomped on his foot *and* shoved a quarter into his muffin. But somehow I convinced myself that it was all Desiree's fault. If she hadn't come along, enticing him with her angelic beauty and harp-playing skills and delicious cookies, Taylor might have been happy with me. Instead, she made me see what I had not been willing to acknowledge before: that Taylor didn't really care about me, and he probably never would.

Yes, I was behaving badly. I admit it.

And, oh, how I hated her! I couldn't stop hating her, and it bothered me. It bothered me so much that one day I went to talk to my bishop. I told him about this girl I hated because she was so beautiful and Taylor wanted to be with her and not with me.

"I just want to stop hating her. I want to stop thinking about her," I told him. "I just don't know how to do it."

My bishop was a very wise man. He cut right to the core of the problem and said, "You're jealous of her. And do you know what jealousy is? It's a lack of self-esteem. I would stop worrying about how you feel about this girl, and think instead about how you feel about yourself."

I think I gasped when he said that, because nobody

had ever been so brutally honest with me before. My bishop saw through me so quickly it was embarrassing. My self-esteem *was* suffering, in a big way. One guy didn't like me as much as I liked him, and because of that I was feeling inadequate and ugly and small.

My self-esteem started to suffer when I started comparing myself to Desiree. It was as if I had held up two pictures, side by side. One picture was of me on my worst day, with the bad haircut I had gotten at the beauty school, the glasses that made me feel nerdy, the figure that was not half as curvy as Desiree's. And the other picture was of Desiree on her best day. She sat at the harp with her cascading long golden hair, capturing every man's heart with her alluring smile.

It's never worth the money you save.

No wonder I felt bad about myself! I had painted myself as the ugly stepsister next to Cinderella. But I have since learned something very important that I wish I had known then. I was not the ugly stepsister. I was not even Cinderella, the scullery-maid-turned-wife-of-the-prince.

I was Prince Charming's sister. You know—a real princess. Not through marriage, but by birthright. And— hold on. Are you listening? This is important—So. Are. You.

You, even on your worst days, are divine royalty. You have it all, and being with a guy or not being with a guy doesn't change that. Being un-wanted by one guy, or even by lots of guys, doesn't change that.

Well, my bishop's ad-vice changed everything. I stopped hating Desiree. I stopped stalking Taylor. When I saw him I was polite, but I didn't give myself an opportunity to think about how much I liked him. And then I set about mending my broken heart.

> YOU, EVEN ON YOUR WORST DAYS, ARE DIVINE ROYALTY.

TRUE STORY!

From the day Brandon moved into my neighborhood in eighth grade, I had a major crush on him. For years we walked home from the bus stop together, had snowball fights, drove home together, and teased each other in our Sunday School classes.

His senior year of high school he decided that he would try to go on a hundred dates with at least fifty girls. Surely, I thought, I would be one of the first to be asked out on a date. I waited and waited and waited. He told me all about the dates he went on, and by the end of the year he had indeed asked out fifty girls—but never me.

—M. L.

So I Say to Myself, Remember This: Kindness Begins with Me

Unfortunately, a broken heart can easily lead to a loss of self-esteem. It's easy to think that being rejected means you are undesirable. It's easy to feel that because someone didn't love you, you are unlovable. It's easy to look in the mirror and wonder if things might have turned out differently if you were just a little more . . . (insert your favorite word here): attractive? thin? strong? funny? smart? outgoing? mature? athletic?

Because it's sometimes so easy to feel bad about yourself, it's more important than ever to be very kind to yourself when you're recovering from a broken heart. One way to do this is to make a list of qualities that you like about yourself and read it every day, or ten times a day, or whenever you feel like crying. If you have a hard time coming up with a list, ask someone who knows you well enough to help you. Your friends and family can often see and admire qualities in you that you are not aware of yourself.

One year for a girls' camp activity, the girls in our ward gathered around the campfire. We were each given a piece of paper and a pencil, and then we drew the name of another girl there. We were asked to write down all of the good qualities we knew about that person. The girl who drew my name was someone I had known for a few years, but she was a year younger than I was, so we didn't really do much together. I didn't think she knew me very well, and I wasn't expecting much from her list.

> YOUR FRIENDS AND FAMILY CAN OFTEN SEE AND ADMIRE QUALITIES IN YOU THAT YOU ARE NOT AWARE OF YOURSELF.

When she gave me my list of strengths, I was astonished. She wrote down things that nobody had ever told me, but they were things I really needed to hear. That list made me feel so good. I kept it for years and every time I read it I felt such a tremendous sense of worth.

So ask some people close to you to help you make a list of your good qualities. You might think this is the lamest suggestion possible and that there is no way you're going to go around begging for compliments. But it doesn't have to be like that. Go to your mom or brother or grandma or best friend and say, "Can you please tell me five things that you like about me?"

Sometimes you don't even have to ask that directly. Sometimes you can confide in someone close to you that you're feeling bad about yourself, and they will volunteer the praise that you need. I have a close friend who is divorced, and when she calls and tells me that her ex-husband has made her feel bad about herself, I know what to do. I tell her all of the things that I like about her, and then listen for the smile and relief in her voice. It's not hard for me to help my friend, and it won't be hard for someone who loves you to do the same for you.

Q: What if I don't have my patriarchal blessing yet?

A: Maybe it's time to think about getting one. Not only will your patriarchal blessing include a declaration of your lineage in the house of Israel, but it will also contain personal counsel and direction from the Lord. As you study your patriarchal blessing and follow the counsel it contains, it will provide you with guidance, comfort, and protection.

If you have a patriarchal blessing, read it often. It will probably tell you what some of your talents and strengths are. It can also give you hope for a bright, happy future.

COME ON,
TRY IT!
(YOU'LL FEEL BETTER)

LIST THE QUALITIES
THAT YOU LIKE ABOUT YOURSELF:

_____

_____

_____

_____

_____

_____

_____

_____

_____

_____

_____

_____

_____

_____

SPEND QUALITY TIME WITH YOUR CREATOR

When I am feeling bad about myself, the best thing I can do is spend time with someone who knows me well and loves me well. Out of all the people in my life who fit that description, nobody can come close to the way my Heavenly Father knows me and loves me. He has known me, and you, since before the world was created.

In President Dieter F. Uchtdorf's talk, "The Love of God," he said, "Think of the purest, most all-consuming love you can imagine. Now multiply that love by an infinite amount—that is the measure of God's love for you." Can you fathom such a love?

President Uchtdorf went on to say, "God does not look on the outward appearance. I believe that He doesn't care one bit if we live in a castle or a cottage, if we are handsome or homely, if we are famous or forgotten. Though we are incomplete, God loves us completely.

Though we are imperfect, He loves us perfectly. Though we may feel lost and without compass, God's love encompasses us completely.

"He loves us because He is filled with an infinite measure of holy, pure, and indescribable love. We are important to God not because of our résumé but because we are His children. He loves every one of us, even those who are flawed, rejected, awkward, sorrowful, or broken. God's love is so great that He loves even the proud, the selfish, the arrogant, and the wicked.

> "OUR INFINITELY COMPASSIONATE HEAVENLY FATHER DESIRES THAT WE DRAW NEAR TO HIM SO THAT HE CAN DRAW NEAR TO US."
> –DIETER F. UCHTDORF

"What this means is that, regardless of our current state, there is hope for us. No matter our distress, no matter our sorrow, no matter our mistakes, our infinitely compassionate Heavenly Father desires that we draw near to Him so that He can draw near to us."[1] ← *I love those words.*

If I apply his message to myself, this is what it says to me: God loves me even if I got a hack-job of a haircut at the beauty school. He loves me even if I ate that package of cookies and can't fit into my jeans. He loves me even when I feel as small and hateful as a rock thrown through a window. He loves me more than I can comprehend, and He always will.

After talking to my bishop about how much I hated Desiree, I took a long time walking home. One nice thing about talking to Heavenly Father is that you don't have to be kneeling down to do it. I walked and looked up at the moon and I talked to God.

I told Him about all of the hurt I felt about Taylor not liking me. I told Him how I hated Desiree, and how I felt guilty about it. I told Him that I worried I would never find someone who would love me for who I was. I poured my heart out to Him during that long walk.

I realized as I did so that it had been a long time since I had really talked to my Father in Heaven. I'm not saying I wasn't praying—I said a prayer every night—but my heart wasn't in it. My heart, along with my thoughts, had been thoroughly consumed with Taylor.

But walking home that night and talking to Heavenly Father started something new for me. I turned my heart and my thoughts to Him, and the change in my focus changed me.

Now, don't get me wrong. I'm not saying that one prayer suddenly fixed everything or healed my broken heart.

But I felt as if I had reached a hand up to heaven and my loving Father (and *your* loving Father) had reached a hand down to me. I didn't feel so alone once I was holding His hand. I didn't feel quite as much grief once the warm peace of the Holy Ghost was surrounding me. And even though I didn't know what would happen in the future, I felt hope because I was walking with God.

President Thomas S. Monson said, "Remember that you do not walk alone. . . . As you walk through life, always walk toward the light, and the shadows of life will fall behind you."[2]

If you will spend time with your Heavenly Father, you will be lifted up and filled with His love. And nothing can heal a broken heart better than to be immersed in God's perfect, endless love.

COME ON,
TRY IT!
(YOU'LL FEEL BETTER)

WHAT WOULD YOU TELL
HEAVENLY FATHER IF YOU
COULD TALK TO HIM RIGHT NOW?

TRUE STORY!

We had been dating for a while, and one night we were watching a movie at my apartment and he finally kissed me. It was a kiss that made me tingle all the way to my toes. But shortly after that night, he stopped hanging around with our friends, and he never called me.

I was worried that I had done something wrong, so I texted him. He responded by saying, "The packaging was better than the product. I don't waste my time on girls like that."

I was shocked and hurt and angry that he would treat me that way. I cried a lot. Then I realized that I was a daughter of God and that He loves me. Though it was a very painful breakup, the experience helped me recognize the right guy when he did come along.

—C. F.

FORGIVENESS ISN'T JUST FOR SINS

Whether your heart is broken intentionally or quite by accident, it is easy to turn the pain of rejection into anger at the person who rejected you. The world will tell you that anger is justified and that vengeance is sweet. But the world is wrong.

On my mission in the Philippines, I had a Filipino companion who loved to cook, and I loved to eat her cooking. I had been in the country for only a few weeks when she cooked a meal that included peppers in the sauce.

Now, I'm not talking about red or green or yellow peppers. I'm not even talking about jalapeño peppers. I'm talking about the tiniest, hottest, most brutal pepper known in that part of the world—the *siling labuyo*, or bird's eye chili. Everyone in the Philippines knew they weren't supposed to actually eat the peppers. Except for me. Because, you know, I was in a foreign country and *nobody told me.*

So there I was, happily eating this delicious dinner, when I suddenly bit into a volcano. It was beyond hot. I actually stopped breathing for a minute, it was such a shock. Tears started streaming down my face, and my nose ran like a faucet. I think I even screamed. I grabbed a cup of water and poured it down my throat, but the water just slid right by the heat.

Okay, I know I screamed.

I jumped up and tried in vain to find something—anything—to stop the pain. But there was no antidote in sight. I ran around the kitchen, coughing and gasping and crying all at once. I thought I would die. It hurt so much.

My companion sat there and calmly watched me behave like a lunatic. Then she said, "You know, you're not supposed to *eat* the peppers."

Yeah. Thanks for telling me that—*now*. If she had told me before dinner not to eat the peppers, do you think I would have eaten them? No!

Well, holding onto anger is like putting a wicked-hot pepper in your mouth. It will *hurt*. Since I have lived in the land of broken hearts before, I will give you the warning that I wish someone had given me: don't eat the peppers. Don't even put them in your mouth.

In other words, steer clear of anger. Don't take it in, don't carry it around, and don't make a place for it in your heart.

Anger will eat at the most tender parts of your heart and make you hard-hearted, bitter, and jaded. A hard heart cannot feel the gentle touch of the Holy Ghost. A bitter heart cannot taste the sweetness of forgiveness. A jaded heart cannot believe in Christ's power to heal all wounds.

> HOLDING ONTO ANGER WILL HURT. A HARD HEART CANNOT FEEL THE GENTLE TOUCH OF THE HOLY GHOST.

If you turn your pain to anger, and if you feed that anger and let it harden your heart, you will become separated from the One who would be your constant companion—the Holy Ghost. And the pain of a broken heart will feel like a paper cut compared to the amputation of the Comforter. Your anger will harm you much more than it will ever harm the person you're angry with.

I don't know what the antidote for that pepper was, but I do know the antidote for anger. It is forgiveness. You must forgive the person who broke your heart. Holding onto anger against him just keeps the wound open and raw. Healing comes when we move on and when we change our focus from anger to forgiveness.

But what if you can't forgive the person who hurt you?

If you find it difficult to forgive, you are not alone. It is one of the great challenges of earthly life. Under the law of Moses, it was "an eye for an eye, and a tooth for a tooth" (Matthew 5:38). But when Christ came, He taught a higher law, saying, "Love your enemies, bless them that curse you, do good to them that hate you, and pray for them which despitefully use you, and persecute you" (Matthew 5:44).

It isn't romantic love that this scripture is talking about. It's charity, the pure love of Christ, that you need in order to love your enemies. Sometimes, even though I want to do what this scripture says, I simply don't have the right kind of love in my heart. Sometimes, when I need it most, I discover that my well of ← Have you ever felt that way? charity is bone-dry.

Thankfully, charity is given to us as a gift from heaven. Charity can be poured into our hearts so that we can love the way Christ loves. And the way we receive it is so simple, yet so important.

Mormon wrote that we must "pray unto the Father with all the energy of heart, that [we] may be filled with this love, which he hath bestowed upon all who are true followers of his Son, Jesus Christ" (Moroni 7:48).

So pray with all your heart. Pray for the ability to forgive. Pray for the person who hurt you. Pray to be filled with the love of Christ. And the Lord will fill your well of charity until it overflows. Even if all you have is the desire to forgive the person who hurt you, it is enough to take to the Lord. If you will bring Him the desire, the Lord will provide the miracle of forgiveness.

> PRAY FOR THE ABILITY TO FORGIVE. PRAY TO BE FILLED WITH THE LOVE OF CHRIST. AND THE LORD WILL FILL YOUR WELL OF CHARITY UNTIL IT OVERFLOWS.

Forgiveness can go a long way toward healing a broken heart. Forgiveness can keep the experience from becoming baggage that you carry around with you. Forgiveness can help you look past the pain of the ending and remember the happiness of the beginning again. Forgiveness can open your heart to love again, and to *be* loved again. So start forgiving today. Right now.

THE ATONEMENT ISN'T JUST FOR SINNERS

There is only so much you can do on your own to mend your broken heart. Some wounds are simply beyond mortal help. But you can draw on the healing power of the Atonement to heal your heart.

Elder Jeffrey R. Holland spoke eloquently on this subject when he said, "I speak to those who are facing personal trials and family struggles, those who endure conflicts fought in the lonely foxholes of the heart, those trying to hold back floodwaters of despair that sometimes wash over us like a tsunami of the soul. I wish to speak particularly to you who feel your lives are broken, seemingly beyond repair.

"To all such I offer the surest and sweetest remedy that I know. It is found in the clarion call the Savior of the world Himself gave . . . :

"'Come unto me, all ye that labour and are heavy laden, and I will give you rest.

"'Take my yoke upon you, and learn of me; for I am meek and lowly in heart: and ye shall find rest unto your souls.'"

Elder Holland continues by saying, "I testify that the Savior's Atonement lifts from us not only the burden of our sins but also the burden of our disappointments and sorrows, our heartaches and our despair. . . . When [Christ] says to the poor in spirit, 'Come unto me,' He means He knows the way out and He knows the way up. He knows it because He has walked it. He knows the way because He *is* the way.

"Brothers and sisters, whatever your distress, *please* don't give up and *please* don't yield to fear. . . .

"If you are lonely, please know you can find comfort. If you are discouraged, please know you can find hope. If you are poor in spirit, please know you can be strengthened. If you feel you are broken, please know you can be mended."[3]

I love that message, especially the last line: "If you feel you are broken, please know you can be mended." Christ can mend anything and everything. He has conquered all pain, all sin, all illness, and even all heartache. There is no wound too great or

That is so true! →

too trivial to take to the Savior for healing. You can come unto Christ and be healed through His Atonement.

How do you come unto Christ? The answers are so simple you probably learned them in Primary. But think about them as if hearing them for the first time.

Come unto Him by hearing the words of prophets, both ancient and modern. Study the scriptures and listen to the counsel of our prophet today.

> THERE IS NO WOUND TOO GREAT OR TOO TRIVIAL TO TAKE TO THE SAVIOR FOR HEALING.

Come unto Him by partaking of the sacrament worthily every week. Remember your covenants to always remember Him and to keep His commandments.

Come unto Him by striving to be like Him, by keeping Him in your thoughts and in your heart each day.

Come unto Him by believing He has the power to heal you. Ask Him to heal you. Pray for the miracle of the Atonement to change your heart.

The Savior wants you to come unto Him. He wants to give you His comfort, His easy yoke, His love and peace. So come unto Christ.

COME ON, TRY IT! (YOU'LL FEEL BETTER)

WRITE DOWN YOUR OWN IDEAS FOR HOW YOU CAN COME UNTO CHRIST.

_____

_____

_____

_____

_____

_____

_____

WRITE DOWN YOUR FAVORITE SCRIPTURE ABOUT COMING UNTO CHRIST.

_____

_____

_____

_____

_____

RULE #4

LOOK TO THE FUTURE

Let's review how far we've come on this journey to mend your broken heart. You've avoided acting pathetic, desperate, neurotic, or creepy. You've forgiven the person who hurt you. You've drawn closer to the Lord and asked for the healing power of the Atonement. So now what?

Now is the time to look to the future. Here are some ways to do that:

1. Look for the positive.

2. Improve yourself.

3. Serve others.

4. Begin new relationships.

5. Evaluate the experience.

ACCENTUATE THE POSITIVE

A popular song during the 1940s encouraged people to "accentuate the positive" and "eliminate the negative." I think if any generation had a good reason to feel despair, it would be those who lived through World War II. So if they can sing about accentuating the positive, so can you. No matter what your broken heart has done to you, you can find a way to accentuate the positive.

My dad has a favorite saying for when things are less than perfect. He'll say, "Well, it's better than a poke in the eye." And do you know what? There are a lot of things in life that are better than a poke in the eye. Seriously, that would hurt!

You might be thinking, "Oh, yeah? I think a broken heart hurts worse than a poked eye." But stop and consider that getting poked in the eye could make you blind. Forever. But a broken heart doesn't have to last forever.

It can be mended, and it can return to wholeness. So maybe—just maybe—a broken heart *is* better than a poke in the eye.

But whether a broken heart really is better than a poke in the eye all depends on your attitude about it.

Here's a little exercise to help you realize the difference your attitude can make on your emotions. Say, "My life is terrible. I hate everything about it." Say it a couple of times, out loud, and I bet pretty soon you will feel your spirit start to sink and darken. Now say, "My life is great. I have so much to look forward to." Say it a few more times, and I bet you will feel the corners of your mouth start to turn up and your spirit lighten. We have so much control over our attitude, and our attitude has so much control over our future.

So say positive things to yourself every day. If you want, write down some sayings that help you feel positive and tape them on your mirror or by your bed or on the fridge. They could be sayings like, "My life is great!" or "I am *so* not the ugly stepsister!" or "Happy days will come again!" If you train your mind what to think, it will soon start thinking those things on its own. Before you know it, you could be thinking, "Well, it's better than a poke in the eye." And you will probably be right!

> IF YOU STAY POSITIVE AND BELIEVE IN BETTER DAYS, THEY WILL COME—AND PROBABLY SOONER THAN YOU THINK.

It might be difficult right now to believe that you will be happy again. Sometimes in the middle of a cold, snowy winter, I find it impossible to imagine ever being too hot. But six months later, in the middle of a hot summer, I find it impossible to imagine ever being too cold. Most of us live so concretely in the here and now that it is hard for us to really believe in the changes of the future. But if you stay positive and believe in better days, they will come—and probably sooner than you think.

COME ON, TRY IT!
(YOU'LL FEEL BETTER)

IT'S BETTER THAN A POKE IN THE EYE...

Make up your own saying, like "It's better than a slap in the belly with a wet fish."

"It's better than . . ."

_____

_____

_____

_____

WRITE A LIST OF POSITIVE SAYINGS YOU WANT TO POST AROUND THE HOUSE.

_____

_____

_____

_____

_____

_____

IMPROVEMENT AND PROGRESSION ARE ONE ETERNAL ROUND

How do you accentuate the positive? Improve yourself. Begin a new project. Develop a talent. Start a hobby. Run for student council. Take music lessons. Organize a club.

Why? Because anything that you do to improve yourself is a wise investment. For one thing, it will take your mind off your pain while you're waiting for your broken heart to heal. For another, it will help you develop as a person. It will add another facet to your personality. It will make you more interesting and give you something new to talk about. It might even give you opportunities to meet new people and form

Q: What exactly is a facet?

A: Facets are flat faces on geometric shapes. Gemstones often have facets cut onto them to improve their appearance by allowing them to reflect more light.

new friendships. All of these things will help you in the process of mending your heart.

Remember the rule about like attracting like? If you have goals and are doing great things, you will attract other people who also have goals and are also doing great things.

Sometimes developing a talent is as easy as picking up a book at the library and teaching yourself a new skill. I have a friend who taught himself how to program video games

> **IF YOU HAVE GOALS AND ARE DOING GREAT THINGS, YOU WILL ATTRACT OTHER PEOPLE WHO ALSO HAVE GOALS AND ARE ALSO DOING GREAT THINGS.**

that way. You can learn just about anything that way— for example, how to speak French, how to play the guitar, how to arrange flowers, or how to do magic tricks.

If you have some money that you can spend on a class, check out your local continuing education program. Most cities offer affordable classes in a variety of subjects. I have loved my city's continuing education program. I pay a modest fee and go once a week, usually in the evening. Some of the classes I have taken include ballet, drawing, storytelling, and calligraphy. And they also offer classes in self-defense, Spanish, and cooking, along with many others. And you don't have to go by yourself—invite a friend to go with you.

MY FAVORITE COOKIES

1 cup butter
1 cup white sugar
1 cup brown sugar
2 eggs
1 teaspoon vanilla
2½ cups oats
2 cups flour
1 teaspoon baking soda
1 teaspoon baking powder
½ teaspoon salt
2 cups chocolate chips
(I like semisweet but milk chocolate is good too)

Which may or may not be better than Desiree's

Preheat oven to 350 degrees. In a large bowl, cream together butter, white sugar, brown sugar, eggs, and vanilla. Set aside. Grind the oats in a blender. Set aside. In a separate bowl, mix the dry ingredients together and add the ground oats. Add dry ingredients to the wet ingredients. Stir in chocolate chips. Drop by spoonfuls onto cookie sheet. Bake for 8 to 10 minutes.

Makes about 2 dozen cookies

You may know someone in your ward who is good at something and who might be willing to teach you. I decided one time to try to make a quilt. I was so grateful for an experienced neighbor who helped me decipher the instructions and knew what to do when I panicked because I had cut all the corners too small. You probably have neighbors and ward members who have a lot of different skills. Look around you and start asking people what they do for fun.

You may be surprised at what you learn.

You, in turn, will become more interesting. People like to be friends with interesting people who have interesting things to talk about. So make yourself interesting. Read books. Try a new sport. Watch the cooking channel and make one of the recipes. You will be happier the more you engage in productive activities.

Focusing on your own improvement can take your mind off your broken heart, give you something new to think about and work toward, and offer you opportunities to feel good about who you are. So improve and progress.

COME ON, TRY IT! (YOU'LL FEEL BETTER)

TALENTS AND HOBBIES:

What are some skills you would like to develop? What hobbies are you interested in? What talents do you admire in the people around you?

WHEN WE'RE HELPING
WE'RE HAPPY

Another way you can take your mind off your own heartache and sorrow is by reaching out to help others. If you do, you will find that there are a lot of people who have trials that are worse than your broken heart. When you forget yourself in service to others, you will feel better about yourself. You will invite the Spirit into your heart when you serve selflessly. You will feel good about how you have spent your time, and your happiness will be reflected in the way you interact with others.

Do you know the hymn, "A Poor Wayfaring Man of Grief"? The lyrics describe a man who serves others, both with small acts, like giving someone food, and with great acts, like giving up his life. Even though he sacrifices something to the one he is serving, in every instance he is blessed with more than he gives. He gives up his food, but his crust of bread tastes like manna to him. He gives up his bed and sleeps on the earth, but it seems like the Garden of Eden. I think the fifth verse of the hymn is especially appropriate.

> Stript, wounded, beaten nigh to death,
> I found him by the highway side.
> I roused his pulse, brought back his breath,
> Revived his spirit, and supplied
> Wine, oil, refreshment—he was healed.
> I had myself a wound concealed,
> But from that hour forgot the smart,
> And peace bound up my broken heart.[4]

President Gordon B. Hinckley, speaking to the youth, said, "There are opportunities all around to stretch our lives and our interests in behalf of others. My plea is—if we want joy in our hearts, if we want the Spirit of the Lord in our lives, let us forget ourselves and reach out. Let us put in the background our own personal, selfish interests and reach out in service to others."[5]

Your service to others can come in the form of an organized service project, but it doesn't have to. And it doesn't have to take a lot of time. If you approach the world each day with a spirit of service, you will find opportunities to serve. It might be opening a door for someone or raking your elderly neighbor's lawn. You might feel prompted to call a young family in your ward and offer to babysit for free so the parents can go on a date.

It can be something big that you organize and devote a lot of time to, like making baby blankets for the hospital or putting together hygiene kits for the Church's Humanitarian Center. A very uplifting act of service is going to the temple and doing baptisms for the dead.

The size of the service really doesn't matter. What matters is that you look outside of yourself and beyond your own troubles. Little by little, your unselfish actions will help to mend your own broken heart.

> "IF WE WANT JOY IN OUR HEARTS, IF WE WANT THE SPIRIT OF THE LORD IN OUR LIVES, LET US FORGET OURSELVES AND REACH OUT."
> –GORDON B. HINCKLEY

COME ON, TRY IT!
(YOU'LL FEEL BETTER)

SERVICE IDEAS:

Make a list of ways you can offer service. Remember to include both large and small acts of service.

THIS MAY BE THE BEGINNING OF A BEAUTIFUL FRIENDSHIP

When you're getting over someone, one of the best ways to feel hopeful about relationships in general is to start a new relationship. But don't do it because you think *he* might see you and be jealous and want you back. If he's the kind of guy who would want you because you're with someone else, then you don't want him. There is no self-respect in winning a guy back that way. But do start new relationships because you can, because it will take your mind off your broken heart, and because it will help you feel better about yourself.

After Zack broke up with me, I let myself feel sad for a few days. And then I got sick of sitting around

Q: What classic movie does the title of this chapter come from?

A: *Casablanca*, and it is a very romantic movie, even though it's in black and white and doesn't have any vampires in it.

feeling sad. There was a play at school that I wanted to see, so I invited one of my guy friends. I didn't ask him out because I wanted a new boyfriend. I just wanted to do something fun with someone I liked. It helped me get over

Of course, I wouldn't have minded, either. (Having a new boyfriend, that is.)

that really painful beginning of a broken heart. I enjoyed myself at the play, I remembered that there were many more people I wanted to get to know, and I didn't spend the evening crying and singing love songs.

> EVEN A NEW OR RENEWED FRIENDSHIP CAN HELP HEAL A WOUNDED HEART.

It doesn't have to be a date, either. Even a new or renewed friendship can help heal a wounded heart.

A new friendship can offer you something new to think about and someone new to talk to. Sometimes even a little change like that can ease the sense of boredom and loneliness that often accompanies a breakup. So get out there and start investing in other relationships.

COME ON, TRY IT! *(YOU'LL FEEL BETTER)*

GET OUT THERE!

Make a list of activities you can do in the next few days and who you want to do them with. Then start inviting people.

ACTIVITY:

INVITATION LIST:

EXPERIENCE IS A MASTER TEACHER

Once you have achieved some distance from your broken heart, try to stand back and assess the experience. This is a great opportunity to ask yourself some pointed questions and to answer them honestly. Some questions you might want to ask yourself include, "What did I do in this relationship that was good or helpful?" And, "What did I do in this relationship that was harmful or hurtful?"

Then think about what changes you want to make for your next relationship. I'm not suggesting that you fundamentally change who you are just so someone will want to be with you. But every relationship will offer you an opportunity to grow and to learn things about yourself. As you grow with each experience, you will recognize behavior and

actions that are immature or small or hurtful. Those are the things you should try to change as part of the maturing process.

For example, I learned from my experience with Zack not to get the relatives involved. I learned from my experience with Taylor not to stalk a guy and that if he doesn't ask me out, it means he's not interested. I have had my

> EVERY RELATIONSHIP WILL OFFER YOU AN OPPORTUNITY TO GROW AND TO LEARN THINGS ABOUT YOURSELF.

heart broken many times, and each time I learned something new. I'm glad now for all of the relationships I had before I met my husband, because each one made me a little better, a little more mature, and a little bit wiser.

A Chinese scholar wrote, "The gem cannot be polished without friction, nor man perfected without trials." God gives us trials to polish us like gems. Sometimes trials can chip away at our faults, like our pride or selfishness. Sometimes trials can smooth our rough edges by softening our hearts and making us more compassionate.

After suffering for months in Liberty Jail, Joseph Smith was told by the Lord, "All these things shall give thee experience, and shall be for thy good" (D&C 122:7). Hopefully your suffering will not be as long or as devastating as the Prophet's suffering. But even if it is, you can take heart and apply the Lord's consolation to your own situation. This experience can be for your good, if you will look for the good in it.

COME ON, TRY IT! (YOU'LL FEEL BETTER)

WHAT DID I DO IN THIS RELATIONSHIP THAT WAS GOOD OR HELPFUL?

_____

_____

_____

_____

_____

_____

WHAT DID I DO IN THIS RELATIONSHIP THAT WAS HARMFUL OR HURTFUL?

_____

_____

_____

_____

_____

ARE WE THERE YET?

We have come a long way together, haven't we? Could there possibly be anything more to say on this subject? Haven't we considered everything? Well, yes, except for one thing, and it's this: if it gets bad, get help.

If you feel like you can't find anything to live for, this is not normal. If after a few weeks, and if after following the rules I talked about, you still feel despair and hopelessness, it's more than a broken heart. It's probably depression, and you should get help. There should be sunshine after rain, not rain upon endless rain.

> THERE SHOULD BE SUNSHINE AFTER RAIN, NOT RAIN UPON ENDLESS RAIN.

Talk to your parents, a church leader, your school counselor, or your doctor. Or better yet, talk to all of them. Talking is important when you feel like life holds no happiness for you. Asking for help is important too, because it is easy in the middle of despair to feel very alone.

I know. I've been there.

But you are not alone! You have an all-powerful, divine, perfect Father in Heaven watching you, loving you, and wanting you to be happy. You deserve to be happy. You really do. So ask someone for help if you need it. There's no shame in it, I promise.

A Final Thought

Now can I tell you one last thing? I believe in you. I believe that you are amazing. I believe that in this life you will be loved deeply and without end.

So put a smile on your face and continue your journey to mend your broken heart.
There is a great life ahead of you.

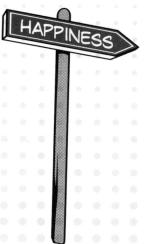

Love,

Julie

ACKNOWLEDGMENTS

Thanks to the creative geniuses at Deseret Book for making this book better than I dreamed: to Lisa Mangum for her stellar editing; Heather Ward for the killer cover and design; Bryan Beach for his awesome illustrations; Heidi Taylor for general hand-holding (but not literally); and Chris Schoebinger for his vision and mentoring.

Thanks to Ally Condie, the matchmaker, for convincing me to write this.

Thanks to my first readers, for their feedback and enthusiasm: Marla Kucera, Julie Dixon, Ally Condie, Pam Anderton, Jaime Mormann, and my mom.

Thanks to my photographer and friend Erin Summerill, who uses her superpowers for good (mostly) and not evil.

Thanks to the Donaldson clan, both near and far, for cheering me on.

ACKNOWLEDGEMENTS

Thanks to my parents, for everything, but especially for teaching me how to laugh at myself. To Kristi, Jenny, Audrey and Nick, for laughing with me, or crying, as needed.

A special thanks to Freddie, for his support and love, and to my kids, Adah, David, Sarah, and Jacob, for giving me joy.

ENDNOTES

1. Dieter F. Uchtdorf, "The Love of God," *Ensign,* November 2009, 22–23.

2. Thomas S. Monson, "On Being Spiritually Prepared: Counsel from our Prophet," *Ensign,* February 2010, 6.

3. Jeffrey R. Holland, "Broken Things to Mend," *Ensign,* May 2006, 69, 70–71; emphasis in original.

4. James Montgomery, "A Poor Wayfaring Man of Grief," in *Hymns of The Church of Jesus Christ of Latter-day Saints* (Salt Lake City: The Church of Jesus Christ of Latter-day Saints, 1985), no. 29.

5. Gordon B. Hinckley, "Words of the Prophet: Forget Yourself and Serve," *New Era,* July 2006, 5.